little grasshopper books™

100
words
on the farm

Get the App!

1. Download the Little Grasshopper Library App* from the App Store or Google Play. Find direct links to store locations at **www.littlegrasshopperbooks.com**

2. Wait for the app to Install and open it.

3. Tap the **+ Add Book** button at the bottom of the screen.**

4. Line up the QR Code Scanner with the QR Code found below.

5. Your book will automatically start downloading to your app!

6. Be sure to accept any prompts that come up.

7. Information on device compatibility and troubleshooting can be found at **www.littlegrasshopperbooks.com**

*We reserve the right to terminate the apps.
**Smartphone not included. Standard data rates may apply to download. Once the app and an individual book's content are downloaded, the app does not use data or require Wi-Fi access.

pitchfork

boots

hat

farmer

jeans

shirt

barn

owl

cat

cricket

mouse

hay

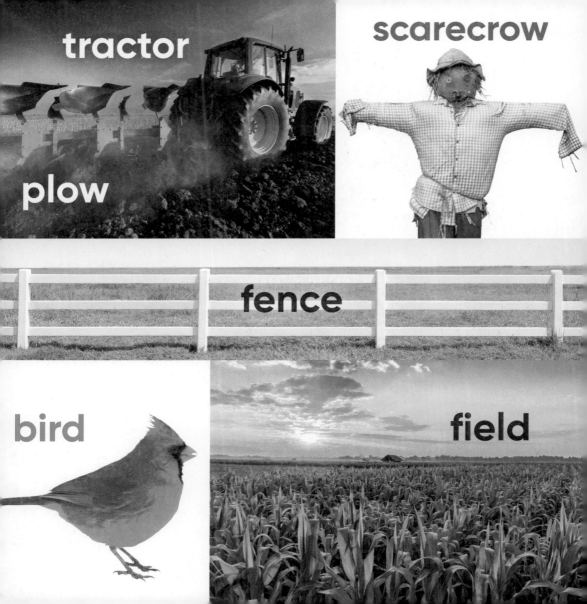

tractor

scarecrow

plow

fence

bird

field

calf

cow

bull

milk

pail

chew

mane

horse

gate

foal

hoof

wheelbarrow

hoe

crop

corn

rake

spade

rain

sun

sunflower

wheat

grasshopper

grow

lamb

sheep

ewe

herd

jump

goat

dog

wool

ram

kid

eat

pen

duck

duckling

frog

pond

turkey

splash

peck

rooster

egg

hen

chickens

chick

tail

pig

sty

mud

piglet

fly

hog

snout

sow

potato

tomato

radish

lettuce

garden

carrot

beans

ant

bug

bee

beehive

ladybug

pear

seed

peach

fruit

apple

tree

bale

silo

windmill

cloud

ribbon

fair

market

prize